Crazy Canadian Trivia 3

D0878672

Scholastic Canada Ltd.
604 King Street West, Toronto, Ontario M5V 1E1, Canada

Scholastic Inc.
557 Broadway, New York, NY 10012, USA

Scholastic Australia Pty Limited
PO Box 579, Gosford, NSW 2250, Australia

Scholastic New Zealand Limited
Private Bag 94407, Greenmount, Auckland, New Zealand

Scholastic Children's Books
Euston House, 24 Eversholt Street, London NW1 1DB, UK

Library and Archives Canada Cataloguing in Publication
Hancock, Pat
Crazy Canadian trivia 3 / Pat Hancock ; illustrations by Bill Dickson.
ISBN 978-0-545-99995-3
1. Canada--Miscellanea--Juvenile literature. I. Dickson, Bill II. Title.
III. Title: Crazy Canadian trivia three.
FC58.H284 2008   j971   C2007-907184-8

ISBN-10 0-545-99995-2

6 5 4 3 2 1   Printed in Canada   08 09 10 11 12 13

Pat Hancock

Crazy Canadian Trivia 3

Illustrations by Bill Dickson

Scholastic Canada Ltd.

Toronto New York London Auckland Sydney
Mexico City New Delhi Hong Kong Buenos Aires

To Brendan Wheeler, a supportive ten-year-old who kept asking me, "How's that new book coming along?" and who ran up and gave me a big hug when I finally answered, "It's done!"

Introduction

I love coming across amazing, cool, wild, wacky,
wonderful and just plain silly facts about Canada
and Canadians. When I do, I usually collect them.
I tuck clippings about them into folders and
I store files and bookmarks about them on my
computer. I also like sharing them because I
figure somebody else may think they're interesting
or entertaining too. In this case, I hope you are
that somebody, and that you'll have fun reading
this latest batch of trivia I've pulled from
my files.

Pat Hancock

Huggable High

On April 23, 2004, students, staff, parents and other friends of St. Matthew's Catholic High School in Orleans, Ontario — 5117 bodies in all — gathered outside the building. Crowding together in a huge circle, they all reached out and hugged one another. After 10 seconds they broke apart, cheering. They had just set a record — for the largest group hug in the world.

The King of the Castles

Harrison Hot Springs, at the southern tip of Harrison Lake in British Columbia, is a popular tourist destination. Its Fraser Valley scenery is spectacular, the two hot springs attract people who like bathing in steamy, mineral-filled pools, and swimmers, sailors and windsurfers enjoy the sandy beach all summer long.

But the main tourist draw for a few weeks each year is the beach sand itself. It's the best kind of sand for building sandcastles because it really sticks together

when it's wet and packed down. So every September some of the world's best sand sculptors come to Harrison Hot Springs to take part in the World Championship of Sand Sculpture.

Competitors spend up to three days carving out "sand-tastic" sea monsters, oversized cars, towering statues and fanciful castles — whatever they're inspired to create. When they're done, the beach becomes a gallery for the biggest outdoor art show in western Canada. And without tides or rolling waves to wash them away, the amazing sculptures stay on the beach until Thanksgiving Day.

He said What?

"When you're a short actor you stand on apple boxes, you walk on a ramp. When you're a short star everybody else walks in a ditch."
— Michael J. Fox

Fox, the star of many TV series and films, was born in Edmonton, Alberta. He is 162 centimetres (5'4") tall.

The Fastest Ice in the World

That's the claim to fame of the covered speed-skating oval built for the Winter Olympics held in Calgary, Alberta, in 1988.

The ice on the 400-metre-long track is carefully maintained to make sure that world champion skaters zipping around it have the smoothest, hardest ice on which to achieve record-breaking speeds. The temperature, humidity and air flow inside the building are also carefully controlled to ensure that the exceptionally high quality of the ice remains the same during competitions watched by thousands of heat- and moisture-generating fans.

So from 1988 until 2002, when the Winter Olympics were held in Salt Lake City, Utah (USA), most world speed-skating records were broken at Calgary's Olympic Oval. Then, for a few years, the track in Salt Lake City claimed to have the fastest ice, and rightly so. But as of March 2007, Salt Lake was the site of just 10 record-breaking skates, whereas 12 current world records were set in Calgary, making it once again home to the fastest ice in the world.

One Land, Many Voices

Canada has two official languages, English and French. Our provinces and territories, however, are all over the map. Quebec has one official language: French. New Brunswick is the only province with two official languages: English and French. The other provinces have not made any languages official, nor has Yukon Territory, but the territory of Nunavut has three official languages: English, French and Inuktitut.

And the Northwest Territories? Beneath the snowflake-inspired crown atop the mace, or ceremonial rod, that symbolizes the government's authority are the words "One land, many voices" — showing how committed the government is to respecting *all* the languages used by its people. So the Northwest Territories has 11 official languages: English, French, Chipewyan, Cree, Gwich'in, Inuktitut, Inuinnaqtun, Inuvialuktun, North Slavey, South Slavey and Dogrib.

Riding High in Thunder Bay

On July 1, 2003, Thunder Bay, Ontario, resident Brad Graham rode his bicycle around the parking lot of Thunder Bay's community auditorium and into the *Guinness World Records* book. He didn't ride very far and he didn't ride very fast, but he did ride very high above the ground. Graham's homemade SkyCycle was a wonderfully wacky creation that measured 4.34 metres from the top of its handlebars to the bottom of its two standard bike wheels, setting a record for the world's tallest rideable bicycle.

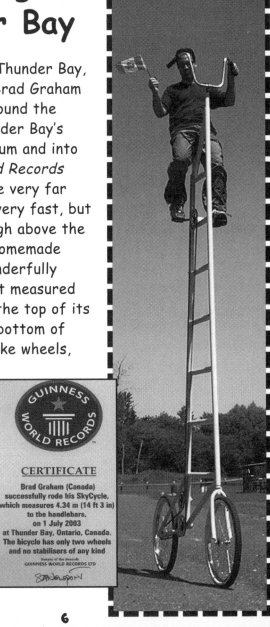

GUINNESS WORLD RECORDS

CERTIFICATE

Brad Graham (Canada)
successfully rode his SkyCycle,
which measures 4.34 m (14 ft 3 in)
to the handlebars,
on 1 July 2003
at Thunder Bay, Ontario, Canada.
The bicycle has only two wheels
and no stabilisers of any kind

Keeper of the Records
GUINNESS WORLD RECORDS LTD

Riding Higher
in Winnipeg

Not to be outdone, on June 26, 2004, Terry Goertzen, a Mennonite church pastor in Winnipeg, Manitoba, rode even higher. Like Brad Graham, Goertzen loved building zany bikes, and the one that he rode 300 metres to qualify for the World's Tallest Bike record was 5.5 metres high. Goertzen's bicycle was similar to Graham's, with the main frame forming a ladder up to the seat. The chain that drove the wheels was 11 metres long!

HOW short Is It?

When a crop is especially poor, some folks in Saskatchewan say:

"*This year the crop's so short that the gophers have to kneel to eat.*"

That's short!

DID YOU KNOW...

...that the first woman to fly a plane in Newfoundland was the great American aviator Amelia Earhart?

In 1928, when Earhart became the first woman to cross the Atlantic by plane, she and two other pilots, William Stultz and Lew Cordon, took off from Trepassey, Newfoundland. And four years later, on May 20, 1932, when she set out on her historic solo flight across the Atlantic Ocean — becoming the third person and the first woman to do so — she again took off in Newfoundland, this time from Harbour Grace. On board she carried a Thermos of hot soup made by a local resident, Rose Archibald.

Round and Round She Goes

Wendy Killoran, a mother and schoolteacher from London, Ontario, also chose Newfoundland as the starting point of a challenging journey. It was also where she ended it.

A keen kayaker since 1991, Killoran set out from Isle Aux Morts, Newfoundland, on May 5, 2006. One hundred and four days later, after kayaking 2700 kilometres, she paddled back to shore at Isle Aux Morts, becoming the first woman to circumnavigate, or go all the way around, Newfoundland.

A year earlier, Killoran also became the first woman to kayak around an entire province — Prince Edward Island — and in 2004, she paddled around the world's largest freshwater island — Manitoulin Island in Lake Huron.

What's in a Name?

Plenty, if you're Cecil Nesmo, a rancher near Manyberries, a small town in the badlands of southern Alberta. For nearly 60 years, researchers had been visiting the Nesmo family's property looking for — and finding — fossils. After all, this was dinosaur country, and Nesmo never turned away a genuine dinosaur hunter. That's why, in 2001, he was more than willing to let Michael Ryan, a graduate student of paleontology (prehistoric life) from the University of Calgary, camp out on his property to examine some very old exposed bones. Those bones would turn out to be part of the skeleton of a type of dinosaur no one had ever seen before.

Tests would later reveal that the "new" dinosaur was very old — about 78 million years old — and that it was a member of the ceratops family. But as well as having the huge horns of dinosaurs like triceratops, the skull also had a large spiked collar, or frill, a lot like those found on another group of ceratops called centrosaurs. The combination of these two features had never before been found on one dinosaur.

It took Ryan a few years to finish studying his exciting discovery of a new kind of dinosaur, but when he proudly published the news of his find in a scientific journal, he also announced to the world the name he had given it — *Albertaceratops nesmoi*. When Cecil Nesmo heard the news, he was surprised and honoured. He had never dreamed when he let Ryan camp out on his ranch that one day he would have a dinosaur named after him.

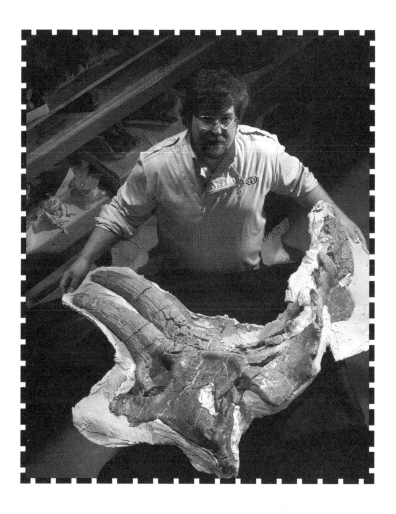

It's a Blockbuster!

When the Canadian National Exhibition (also known as the CNE or the Ex) opened on Friday, August 17, 2007, in Toronto, Ontario, visitors were invited to join in the fun of building the world's tallest tower — out of Lego blocks!

Over a period of three days, thousands of kids and adults snapped together hundreds of thousands of the small plastic bricks. Guided by engineers from Lego's headquarters in Denmark, they built separate sections that were lifted by workers in the bucket of a large crane and carefully placed securely on top of each other. By Monday the multi-coloured tower was tall enough to make its mark on Toronto's skyline, but no one could say for sure just how tall it was. Strong winds made it too dangerous for the crane to hoist someone up to the top with a tape measure.

Finally, on Wednesday, the measurement was made and it was official — the tower was a record-breaker. At 29.03 metres — about nine storeys tall — the giant four-sided structure was 0.45 metres higher than the previous record holder, a tower built in Carlsbad, California, a few months earlier.

With up to 100 raccoons per square kilometre, Toronto, Ontario, is known as the raccoon capital of North America and maybe even of the world. In rural areas of the province, where you might expect to find more of the masked critters hanging out, the population is just 4 to 12 raccoons per square kilometre.

What's that, eh?

Tarabish, anyone? What is it? It's a card game, often called tarbish, or 'bish, on Cape Breton Island, in Nova Scotia. This is the only place in the whole world where lots of people know how to play the game and absolutely love it. In fact, on March 3, 2007, hundreds of them registered in two-person teams for the 19th annual World Tarabish Championship tournament at the Nova Scotia Community College in Sydney.

He Nailed It!

Allan B. Dove, a chemical engineer who started working for The Steel Company of Canada (Stelco) in Hamilton, Ontario, in the early 1930s, was really interested in nails. Old and new, tiny tacks and big spikes, square-cut and round, he collected them all and studied them carefully, and after years of research, he came up with an idea for a new and improved style of nail.

Dove figured out that a spiral-shaped nail would twist, rather than pound, its way into wood, making hammering it in easier. It would also be less likely to split the wood and would grip it much better than a smooth, round nail. His colleagues at Stelco loved the idea and patented Dove's invention — the ardox nail — in 1954. Ardox nails are now used around the world, and builders have a Canadian to thank.

Just the Stats

On average, Canadians gobble up more than 14 kilograms of bananas every year. Probably some are being eaten on the way to work. Apparently, nearly 40 per cent of Canadians between the ages of 18 and 27 eat breakfast on the run.

Big Time in B.C.

It's 1100 metres above sea level. Its main street looks as though it belongs to a town in the German Alps. German food is on the menu of many of its cafés and restaurants. One of those restaurants is in a 350-year-old Bavarian building — but the building isn't in Bavaria. It was taken apart there and shipped in pieces all the way to British Columbia where it was carefully reassembled in Kimberley, known since the 1970s as "the Bavarian city of the Rockies."

Introducing a German alpine theme to Kimberley was intended to attract more tourists, and the plan worked. Visitors strolling along the Platzl — the German word for the pedestrian mall there — are delighted when Happy Hans pops out of his house to greet them. Hans, who's just 1.2 metres tall, is Kimberley's lederhosen-wearing mascot. Every hour on the hour he steps out on his balcony to yodel for anyone who'll listen. His house is a tourist draw too. Nearly seven metres high, it's the largest working cuckoo clock in North America, and one of the largest in the world. Hans, rather than a cuckoo bird, pops out of it. And if someone wants to see and hear him between scheduled appearances, he's very accommodating. A few coins slipped into a slot are all it takes for him to give a command performance.

Local Flavour

Kimberley's residents have every reason to be proud of their really big cuckoo clock, but the popular German sausages cooked up for visitors there lose out in the bragging department to the Ukrainian sausage in Mundare, Alberta. The 700 or so folks living in this small town east of Edmonton are so proud of the garlic-flavoured, prize-winning kielbasa made at Stawnichy's, the local meat processing plant, that they've erected a monument to it — a 12.8-metre-high fibreglass sausage coil weighing six tons. It's the largest kielbasa in the world!

Riding the River

According to a small but keen group of Montrealers, you don't need to live near an ocean coastline to be able to catch a big wave on a regular basis. You just have to tuck your surfboard under your arm, stroll down to an area behind the housing complex known as Habitat '67, and slip into the swirling waters of the mighty St. Lawrence River near the city's port. It's there you'll find a 30-metre-wide standing, or stationary, wave that surfers love to ride, no matter how cold the water might be.

Just the Stats

By the summer of 2007 more than 80 per cent of Canadians had a cellphone and about 64 per cent of Canadians were checking their e-mail at least once a day.

Look at Me!

Charles Connell, a lumberman born in Carleton County, New Brunswick, in 1810, was a popular politician in that province both before and after Confederation. A strong believer in responsible government, he worked hard on behalf of his constituents right up until his death in 1873. But in 1860 he made a foolish move that left voters wondering, "Charles, what were you thinking?"

In 1859 New Brunswick's lieutenant-governor appointed him postmaster general and asked him to organize the design and production of new 1-, 5-, 10- and 12½-cent stamps. The new stamps were supposed to go on sale on May 1, 1860. But when the lieutenant-governor was sent a set for approval in late April, he was stunned. The five-cent stamp was unacceptable. He had expected to see a portrait of Queen Victoria on it, but that picture had been replaced with one of a man he knew well — none other than Charles Connell himself!

Connell was ordered not to release the stamp on May 1st and to get replacements printed as quickly as possible. He did as he was told, and then quickly resigned as postmaster general. He personally bought all 500 000 copies of the rejected stamps and burned almost all of them,

saving just a few sheets as souvenirs for his daughters and a close friend. Supposedly, his daughters destroyed theirs, not wanting to keep evidence of their father's foolishness, and voters eventually forgave and forgot, electing him as a member of Canada's new Parliament in 1867. But we still don't have the answer to the question they puzzled over in 1860 — "Charles, what were you thinking?"

DID YOU KNOW...

...that on December 7, 1898, Canada issued the world's first Christmas stamp? It was a two-cent stamp bearing a picture of a map of the world, with "XMAS 1898" printed across the bottom of the map. And nearly 100 years later, Canada Post issued the world's first "do-it-yourself" stamps, with a blank space on which you could attach special occasion stickers or draw your own decorations.

Chinook Can't Lose

Back in the 1990s a Canadian-made computer program named Chinook beat the world's best checkers players. But Chinook's creator, Jonathan Schaeffer — a computer science professor at the University of Alberta — wasn't satisfied with having his software earn the checkers champ title. He wanted to make sure that any challengers — human or computer — might be able to come up with a draw against Chinook, but they could never win.

Schaeffer began working on Chinook in 1989. Eighteen years later, in July 2007, after millions of calculations using dozens of computers, he and his team of U of A researchers announced that they had finally achieved that goal: their new and improved version of Chinook can never be beaten.

Why did it take so long to perfect Chinook? After all, checkers seems like a pretty simple game when compared to chess, for example. But there are 500 billion billion possible moves in a checker game! By comparison, there are just 765 possible moves in tic-tac-toe.

DID YOU KNOW...

...that the first Scouts' Apple Day in Canada was held in Saint John, New Brunswick, on January 30, 1932? Eli Boyaner, a local optometrist, came up with the idea of having the Boy Scouts — no girls were allowed back then — hand out apples in exchange for whatever donations people wanted to make to support local scouting activities.

The popular fundraiser now takes place each October when fresh, crisp apples are more readily available and when the weather is usually much nicer than in January. But on that first Apple Day, young Scouts didn't let stinging sleet and pelting rain stop them from handing out about 21 000 apples.

The Great Big Escape

First Shu Mei of Newmarket, Ontario, smelled it when she opened her door one morning in mid-July, 2007. Then she saw it — a huge patty of poop way too big to scoop — on her front lawn. Shu Mei stayed clear of the reeking pile, but she did take a closer look at some of her flowers and a tree in her yard. Clearly, something had been eating them — something big.

Shortly before Shu Mei made her smelly discovery, the 9-1-1 calls had started coming in, but at first dispatchers had trouble believing what they were hearing. People were reporting seeing elephants strolling down the street.

The reports were accurate. The cord feeding an electrified fence around a visiting circus's elephant enclosure had been accidentally unplugged, and two of the three large beasts — Bunny and Susie — had decided to check out the neighbourhood. Susie didn't go far, but Bunny made it to Shu Mei's street and stopped to snack on her plants and fertilize her lawn. Fortunately for all concerned, Bunny and Susie were gentle giants, and their trainers had no problem shepherding them back to the circus grounds. One of the trainers even came back and scooped up the poop from Shu Mei's lawn.

Another Critter on the Lam

In July 1990, a pig that was determined not to become bacon escaped from a slaughterhouse in Red Deer, Alberta. Francis, as someone named him, managed to roam free much longer than Bunny and Susie, the elephants who went walkabout in Newmarket. In fact Francis was on the lam for nearly five months, foraging for food in parks and avoiding several attempts to capture him. The longer he roamed free, the more famous he became, and the more people supported him as if he were the underdog in a sports event.

When he was finally cornered he had earned the affection of so many Red Deer residents that no one dared send him back to the abattoir. As the plaque beside a large statue erected in his honour recounts, "This freedom-loving pig was finally captured and spent his remaining life on a local farm."

Runaway
Balloon

Elephants and pigs on the loose in a Canadian city are newsworthy, but a helium-filled balloon on the run? What's so unusual about that? Don't helium balloons escape every day and drift up, up and away? True, but they aren't huge — 25 storeys high — and they're not carrying a gondola loaded with more than half a million dollars worth of scientific instruments. That one got away on August 24, 1998.

The balloon was the centrepiece of a joint research project involving the Canadian Space Agency, Environment Canada and scientists from several universities and a few private companies. The project was designed to gather important information on the thinning of the stratosphere's ozone layer. The idea was to launch the gigantic balloon from an old air base at Vanscoy, Saskatchewan, on a calm, clear day, letting it float 35 kilometres up through the ozone layer, collecting and sending data back to Earth as it rose. And the balloon did exactly that.

It was launched in the early hours of August 24th, drifted straight up and remained overhead until late in the day when researchers sent it a signal that was supposed to release the gondola and let it parachute gently back to the ground. But the gondola didn't

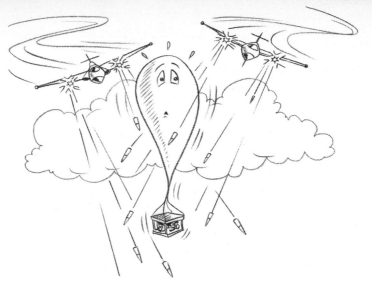

detach. Then the wind came up and the balloon drifted away, heading east over Manitoba and Ontario, toward the St. Lawrence River and into airspace used by commercial flights.

Air traffic controllers were informed of its presence and warned pilots to avoid it. On it sailed, over Quebec and the Maritimes, until two Canadian fighter jets were sent to shoot it down near Newfoundland. But despite being riddled with bullet holes the balloon kept going. American and British fighter planes targeted it too, but they couldn't stop it. Radio and television networks tracked its journey as if it were Santa's sleigh making deliveries on Christmas Eve.

Eventually the balloon entered Russian airspace and, finally, to the relief of everyone involved in the project, on September 2, 1998, it came down in a field on Mariehamn Island, Finland, in the Baltic Sea. Two

Finnish weather scientists located it, packed up the gondola's valuable instruments, and shipped them back to Canada by plane, not balloon. Researchers in Canada were delighted to find that the instruments were still working despite the bullet dents. The project had been much more exciting than they had expected, but it had worked, at least from a data-collection point of view.

They said What?

"The aeroplane is an invention of the devil and will never play any part in such a serious business as the defence of a nation."

— Samuel Hughes, 1914

Sam Hughes was the equivalent of today's minister of defence for Canada from 1911 to 1916, and in many historians' opinions, did a terrible job.

". . . a conceited lunatic."

— Prince Arthur, Duke of Connaught, 1914, referring to Sam Hughes

Prince Arthur, one of Queen Victoria's sons, was Canada's governor general from 1911 to 1916, at the same time as Sam Hughes was the minister in charge of Canada's military.

IT'S A SHOVEL!
IT'S A SHIELD!
IT'S A FLOP

When Sam Hughes's personal secretary, Ena MacAdam, came back from a trip to Switzerland in 1913, she told her boss about a shovel she had seen there that might come in handy for soldiers fighting in the trenches in Europe during World War I. Hughes, after making a few changes in the design, got a patent for the shovel in her name, and ordered nearly 25 000 of them from a steel company in Pennsylvania. Then he shipped at least 22 000 across to Britain to be given to Canadian troops.

The MacAdam shovel, also known as the Hughes shovel, was a short-handled one with a hole in the middle of the blade. Soldiers were supposed to use the shovel as a shield while aiming their rifles through the hole. But Brigadier General McRae was not impressed with the newest piece of equipment to arrive from Canada. He pointed out to his superiors that the hole made it less efficient as a digging tool, and the steel blade and iron handle weighed about 2.3 kilograms, an extra weight that already loaded-down soldiers didn't need to bear.

Besides, the blade wasn't thick enough to stop all bullets and was barely big enough to shield the head. McRae recommended that the 50 tonnes of metal he'd been shipped in the shape of shovels be melted down and put to far better use in fighting the war.

Around 1850 as many as 100 million bison, or buffalo, roamed the Canadian prairies. By about 1880, after just 30 years of overhunting and settlers moving west, there were only a few hundred left.

...that Hairy Hill, Alberta, is named after itchy buffalo?

Hairy Hill is a small town in northeastern Alberta that started out as a post office and trading post in the 1900s. When settlers first arrived there, some buffalo were still roaming freely in Two Hills County. When these large beasts wanted to get rid of biting insects burrowing into their furry hides, they'd rub up against the many clumps of prickly bushes covering the hillside, leaving the branches covered with strands of brown hair. Until people actually saw the buffalo using the plants as back-scratchers, they weren't sure what to make of the strange-looking shrubs. But one thing they were sure of was that the hill was pretty hairy and they referred to it that way. The name, like the hair, stuck.

As for Brownie Bay and Fudge Lake in Manitoba, no one seems to know how these places got stuck with such sweet names.

A Rookie's Nightmare

In 1985-86 rookie defenceman Steve Smith was thrilled to be playing with the NHL's Edmonton Oilers, a team that included such hockey greats as Paul Coffey and Wayne Gretzky. The Oilers had had a fantastic regular season, and appeared to be heading for their third Stanley Cup championship in a row. But they still had to get past another Alberta team, the Calgary Flames, to make it to the finals.

The best-of-seven series with the Flames was tied 3-3 when the two teams met in Edmonton on April 30, 1986, to play the tiebreaker. The score was tied 2-2 in the third period of the must-win game when Smith tried to clear the puck out of his end. But to his horror he passed the puck across his own net where it hit the stick of Grant Fuhr, the Oilers' goaltender, and bounced into the net.

The game ended 3-2 for the Flames — who went on to lose the final series to the Montreal Canadiens. And although the closest Flames player to the play was credited with the goal, Smith, the other Oilers and the Edmonton fans knew that it was one of their own who had accidentally scored the winning goal — for the wrong team! It was a goal Smith always wanted to forget.

Where's an Invisibility Cloak When You Need One?

During a 1968 NHL hockey game between the Boston Bruins and the St. Louis Blues, it was a player, and not a puck, that went astray, leaving the Blues' Noel Picard — another defenceman — open to friendly razzing for years to come. When Picard's shift on the ice ended, he headed for the open door in the boards and slid onto the bench for a well-earned rest. Then he looked around and saw that he was surrounded by opponents, not teammates. Picard had joined the Bruins' bench.

Stung by the fans' laughter and facing the furious glare of his coach, Picard slipped over the boards and raced to the Blues' bench, but not before the referee saw what he was doing and added to Picard's misery by blowing the whistle and penalizing St. Louis — for having too many men on the ice!

DID YOU KNOW...

...that the small town of Viking, Alberta, is home to one of the most famous families in National Hockey League history? Six of the sons of Grace and Louis Sutter of Viking became NHL players, and when their playing days were over, four of them also went on to become NHL coaches and managers.

To honour the young men who put Viking on the map, the town's arena was decorated with a large mural featuring the talented brothers — Brian, Duane, Rich, Darryl, Brent and Ron Sutter.

Altogether, the Sutter brothers played more than 5000 games in the National Hockey League. And on a per capita basis, the arena in Viking has produced more players who made it to the NHL than any other arena in the world.

Free Food to the Rescue

Built and launched in Liverpool, England, in 1864, the SS *Moravian* safely shuttled passengers and cargo across the Atlantic Ocean for several years. The large, sturdy ship did have one close call sailing from Ireland to Quebec in September 1875, when it rammed into an iceberg. Fortunately, it escaped with just minor damage to its hull and continued on its way.

But on December 30, 1881, as it sailed east from Portland, Maine, in stormy weather, the *Moravian's* luck ran out off Cape Sable, the southern tip of Nova Scotia. The treacherous waters pounding the Cape's

shallow and rocky shores — a graveyard for scores
of ships — claimed the vessel. Thankfully, all its
passengers and crew members made it ashore with
the help of some local people who rowed out to help.

But the lives of those aboard the wrecked ship weren't
the only ones saved that day. It had been a very bleak
year for families living along the Cape coast. Food
supplies had dwindled to the point that several
residents were actually starving, and by Christmas a
few had already died. So the local men who rowed out
to the wreck couldn't believe their eyes when they saw
the ship's cargo. The *Moravian* had been carrying

hundreds of barrels of apples and pickled pork, nearly 30 000 bushels of wheat, about 150 tons of bacon, nearly 50 tons of butter and more than 300 tons of cheese! After everyone was rescued, the men worked until dark salvaging all the food they could — plenty to feed the unfortunate passengers and crew for days, and more than enough to feed their own families for the rest of the winter.

"*The best way to treat a cold is with contempt.*"
— William Osler

Born at Bond Head, Canada West (now Ontario), in 1849, Osler became a world-famous doctor who dramatically changed the way medical students were taught.

Easy Does It

Often a simple idea turns out to be a great one. John Mitchell Lyons came up with one of those simple, great ideas when he was working as a railway clerk in Moncton, New Brunswick.

In the late 1870s, Moncton's train station was a very busy place. Trains were regularly arriving from and departing for several different destinations, and travellers often had to switch trains. But the busier the station got, the harder it was to keep track of luggage and make sure that it and its owners ended up in the same place at the same time.

Like so many other clerks across the country, Lyons often had to bear the brunt of travellers' complaints when they realized their bags were lost. But in 1881 he came up with a solution to the problem — a two-part baggage identification check that could be easily torn in half along a line of perforations. One half went to the passengers and the other was attached to their bags. Lyons patented his invention in 1882. It was such a simple, elegant and workable idea that versions of it are still being used around the world today.

Bear on Board

Being "boatjacked" by a bear was definitely not what Marty Descoteaux, owner of Elliot Lake Outfitters, had in mind when he promised visitors to his company's website "a world-class guided Ontario fishing adventure you will never forget." But that's what happened when he headed out one morning onto Esten Lake in his five-metre-long aluminum boat to see how well the fish were biting.

Fortunately, Descoteaux had no customers along for the ride that morning in July 2006, when a large bear swimming nearby suddenly decided it wanted to come aboard. When the bear reached up to grab the side of the boat, Descoteaux whacked it on the head with an oar, but that didn't stop it. When it pulled itself up and in, Descoteaux abandoned ship and started swimming for shore.

In the meantime the bear was checking out the boat, which was still moving at a slow, trolling speed. But when the hairy pirate bumped into the throttle of the main gas-powered motor, the boat shot forward. Descoteaux watched from shore as his craft headed towards some rocks. When it bumped into them, the bear was thrown into the water. It swam ashore and lumbered off into the woods, but the boat kept going, speeding around and around in circles for nearly half an hour until it ran out of gas.

Descoteaux's Ontario fishing adventure finally ended when he swam out and retrieved his boat. It was certainly an experience he would never forget, and it made for a great story to share with his clients when he took them fishing.

...that in 1940 Sudbury, Ontario, became the first city in Canada to install parking meters on its streets? Vancouver didn't begin installing the coin-hungry timekeepers until 1947, and Montreal held off until 1958.

A Parking Price Freeze

By the 2000s most Canadian cities were gradually replacing coin-operated meters with more efficient ways to collect payments for parking spots. But in Winnipeg, Manitoba, for a few days in the winter of 2007, new solar-powered pay stations gave people a break. When the temperature dropped below −30ºC, their liquid crystal displays froze and they stopped issuing receipts for time paid. Instead of saving the city money the cold-sensitive kiosks cost Winnipeg about $2000 a day. Unlike the city's hardy residents, the new machines couldn't handle the cold.

Just the Stats

In Canadian cities in the 1950s, a nickel could buy an hour of on-street metered parking. By 2006 the average hourly rate had reached $2.25.

DID YOU KNOW...

...that the prairie rattlesnake is the only poisonous snake slithering around the Canadian prairies? About a metre long, this greenish-grey or greenish-brown reptile can be found anywhere from southwestern Saskatchewan and southern Alberta to south-central British Columbia. Southern British Columbia is also home to Canada's only member of the boa family, the rubber boa, a constrictor that swallows its prey whole. But it's less than a metre long, just a tenth of the length of some other boas around the world such as pythons and anacondas, so the prey it swallows is pretty small.

The black rat snake is Canada's largest snake, reaching lengths of up to 2.5 metres. It's only found in southern Ontario. And one province, Newfoundland, doesn't have any naturally occurring snakes. It doesn't have any porcupines, raccoons, groundhogs or skunks either.

NO SNAKES!
NO GROUNDHOGS!
NO RACCOONS!
NO SKUNKS!
NO WAY!

Danger:
Escape Artist at Work

Wowing crowds with death-defying stunts is all part of a day's work for Dean Gunnarson of Winnipeg, Manitoba. What happened on Saturday, June 9, 2007, was no exception. That night about 2000 people attending the Old Tyme Country Fair in Niverville, Manitoba, watched and worried as two large tractors began a tug-of-war with Gunnarson, a captive human link at the centre of the ropes being pulled by the powerful machines.

As the tractors drove in opposite directions, slowly picking up the slack in the long ropes, Gunnarson worked feverishly to dismantle the trap he had set for himself — padlocked chains wrapped around his body and handcuffs clamping his hands together. Just as the rope from one tractor went taut and yanked him sideways, he escaped from the last of his restraints and the ropes. The crowd cheered, relieved that the master magician and escape artist hadn't been ripped apart in front of them.

But back in 1983, on Halloween, the thousands of Winnipeggers who had gathered to watch a young Gunnarson perform one of his earliest dramatic escapes had no cause to cheer. Gunnarson had been chained up, sealed in a coffin and thrown into the Red River. Then something went terribly wrong. Unable to escape his shackles, the young man was submerged in the chilly waters for four minutes before the coffin was pulled from the river and opened to rescue him. By that time, he was unconscious and turning blue.

That event was Gunnarson's closest brush with death, but not his most daring stunt. Over the years and around the world he has performed hundreds of amazing feats before TV cameras and huge crowds of appreciative fans. He has been thrown out of a plane handcuffed, chained and in a straitjacket — with just seconds to escape and open a parachute. He's been covered with chicken meat and dangled in restraints over a pit of dozens of hungry alligators. He's been chained to the tracks as a roller coaster thundered towards him. It's no wonder he's considered a master of the world's most dangerous magic, and one of the best escape artists in the world.

...that in both 2006 and 2007 a Canadian was chosen as the top American college female athlete of the year? Soccer all-star Christine Sinclair of Burnaby, British Columbia, won that award in 2006 while playing for the University of Portland, and Sarah Pavan of Kitchener, Ontario, won it in 2007 for her outstanding efforts on the University of Nebraska's championship volleyball team.

More Cross-Border Stardom

Twice in major league baseball history, a Canadian has been named Most Valuable Player. In 2006 Justin Morneau of New Westminster, British Columbia, a first baseman for the Minnesota Twins, was chosen as the American League's MVP. Nine years earlier, Larry Walker of Maple Ridge, B.C., was the 1997 choice for the National League's MVP while playing for the Colorado Rockies.

The year 2006 was also good for another great athlete from British Columbia — superstar basketball player Steve Nash. In 2006 Nash, who grew up in Victoria, was named the National Basketball Association's MVP for the second year in a row while playing for the Phoenix Suns.

What's that, eh?

There are a lot of jumpers in southern Alberta, Saskatchewan and Manitoba. They're found in New Brunswick, Nova Scotia, Quebec and Ontario too, but there they aren't called jumpers. This is the name given to the white-tailed deer by many people on the prairies, and it's a fitting name for these large herbivorous, or plant-eating, mammals. White-tailed deer are impressively athletic. From a standing start they can spring about 1.8 metres into the air, and from a running start they can soar to nearly 2.5 metres.

Quebec's Anticosti Island in the Gulf of
St. Lawrence is home to about 130 000
white-tailed deer, making it a great place
to visit if one is hoping to spot a jumper or two.

DID YOU KNOW...

...that a Canadian invented processed
cheese?

James Lewis Kraft was born in
Stevensville, a farming community in southern Ontario
near Lake Erie. Growing up on a dairy farm and working
as a clerk in the local grocery store, Kraft became
interested in learning about ways to prevent cheese
from spoiling. In 1903, when he was 29, he moved to
Chicago and began selling cheese to grocery stores. A
few years later four of his brothers joined him in
Chicago and they formed a business called J.L. Kraft and
Brothers. After that Kraft started experimenting with
cooking up batches of melted cheese that wouldn't
quickly spoil or go mouldy, and that could be sold in
small tins. In 1916 he received a patent for the method
he had come up with to produce processed cheese, and
the Kraft brand on cheese soon became one consumers
felt they could trust.

Super Old

A centenarian is someone who lives to be 100 years old. About one in 1000 centenarians lives to celebrate a 110th birthday too, and those who do are referred to as supercentenarians. On September 16, 2001, Julie Winnefred Bertrand of Montreal, Quebec, turned 110 and joined this special group.

Even more special — only one in 15 supercentenarians lives to be 114. Ms. Bertrand did that in September 2005. She even went on to celebrate her 115th birthday in September 2006, and when 116-year-old Elizabeth Bolden from Memphis, Tennessee, died in December 2006, Bertrand became the world's oldest woman and second-oldest person. At that time there were only 77 other verified supercentenarians alive.

Bertrand was born in Coaticook, a town in Quebec's Eastern Townships, not far from the Vermont, USA, border. There she worked most of her adult life as a buyer for a department store. In the 1970s she moved to a nursing home in Montreal. Bertrand never married, but at one time she did date a handsome young lawyer from a nearby town — Louis St. Laurent, who went on to serve as Canada's prime minister from 1948 to 1957.

Bertrand died in her sleep on January 18, 2007, just six days before she would have become the oldest person in the world.

Just the Stats

According to the numbers, Canadians, especially women, are living longer now. In the 1960s fewer than 20 people a year were centenarians when they passed away; in 2004, more than 300 were. The 2006 Canadian census counted 4635 living centenarians, 1510 more than in 1996, and five out of every six of them were women.

50

Man-Eating Mosquito

The town of Upsala, Ontario, northwest of Thunder Bay, must figure there's no point trying to hide the fact that some pretty big, bloodthirsty mosquitoes hang out in the area. Visitors there are met right up front with a monstrous member of that insect clan — a steel and fibreglass creature nearly five metres long. But this mosquito isn't just huge; it's really hungry too. Armed with a knife and a fork, it's just waiting to dig into the 1.8-metre-tall man it's clutching in its long, steely legs.

How Big Are They?

As some Quebecers say:

"*At my grandmother's cottage, the mosquitoes are so big they have to kneel to bite us in the forehead.*"

That's big!

The French-Canadian Connection

Madonna wasn't simply trying to please her fans when she mentioned at a sold-out concert in Montreal in 2006 that she had French-Canadian blood.

Not only was her mother, Louise Fortin, the daughter of Quebecois parents who emigrated to the United States in the late 1900s, but the pop superstar also has some historically impressive ancestors. According to Jonathan Lemire, who checked out Madonna's family tree, Madonna is a direct descendant of Jean-Baptiste Masse, one of the group known as Patriotes who led the Rebellion of 1837 against the corrupt government in charge of Lower Canada (now Quebec) at the time. The main leader of the Patriotes was Louis-Joseph Papineau, a major figure in Canadian history, and Madonna is a descendant of his first cousin.

...that the special water that Madonna drinks and insists on having available backstage wherever she performs is actually spring-fed well water bottled by CJC Bottling Ltd. of Grafton, Ontario?

When some of that plain old Ontario water is sold to Madonna and others by people who claim it has healing powers, the price zooms up to about $8 for a 1.5-litre bottle.

Oprah Winfrey is also a fan of Canadian water. She doesn't believe that the water she chose to support in her magazine, *O*, has any special powers, but she does think it tastes good, is very clean, and is attractively packaged. The water she and many other rich and famous people around the world like so much is bottled under the *1Litre* brand name, and it sells for anywhere from $8 to $11 a litre. The same water, which comes from two wells on property owned by Perry and Cathie Robins of Baltimore, Ontario, sells for less than 50 cents a litre if bought directly from their family business, Mill Valley Natural Spring Water Ltd. Those same two wells supply the Robins family with the water they use every day to wash their dishes, do the laundry, bathe in and flush through their septic system.

She Sure Looks Like Oprah

That's what some people in the small fishing village of Alert Bay, British Columbia, were thinking as they watched the casually dressed woman disembark from a 145-metre-long yacht that had just docked at the port. And they were right. It was Oprah Winfrey, dropping by for a visit organized by the yacht's owner, her host, wealthy British Columbia businessman James Pattison.

The world-famous TV show host — and one of the world's richest women — walked leisurely through the village, stopping to talk with local residents, pose for pictures with them and sign autographs. Word of her surprise visit spread like wildfire, and when Bill Cranmer, 'Namgis First Nation chief, heard the news, he found her and invited her to a special celebration being held at the community's Big House. Oprah accepted his invitation and joined about 800 people gathered in and around the cedar lodge. She spoke to the cheering crowd and joined some of them in a drum dance. In turn, the 'Namgis people honoured her by giving her a special name, Noxxolagap, which means a wise and knowledgeable person.

Everyone who met Oprah that day in August 2007 certainly saw her as wise and knowledgeable — and very friendly too.

The Ice Patch Moccasin

In 2003 Cody Joe, a member of the Champagne and Aishihik First Nations, was working with an archaeological research team examining melting ice patches in the southern Yukon. The team was looking for early evidence of aboriginal peoples' presence in the area, so it was especially fitting that Cody Joe was the one who came across the brown, dirt-covered clump of animal hide that the researchers would find so interesting. Moss was growing out of it and it was covered with animal dung, but over the next two years Yukoner Valery Monahan worked for nearly 250 hours carefully cleaning, reconstructing and preserving the item. In February 2006 the territory's Ministry of Tourism and Culture was proud and pleased to announce an amazing discovery. What Cody Joe had found was a 1400-year-old moccasin — the oldest example of a First Nations moccasin ever found in Canada. The leather footwear was probably sewn together and worn by early Athapaskan people.

The Minister's
New Shoes

The minister of finance is an important member of Canada's Parliament in Ottawa. Every year or so, it is his duty to present the budget — the government's major plans for spending taxpayers' money — in a speech in the House of Commons. Many Canadians think that, traditionally, he wears a new pair of shoes for the occasion. But is this true?

Researchers at the Library of Parliament spent a long time trying to get to the bottom of things, but came up empty-handed. They couldn't find when or why the new-shoe idea began, or any evidence that it had been around for very long. In fact, the library's research showed that the first time a newspaper reported that a minister of finance wore new shoes to present a budget was when Jean Chrétien did in 1978. Before that, all the way back to 1946, no minister of finance wore new shoes on budget day. And for the 26 budget speeches from 1978 until the spring of 2007, finance ministers wore new shoes just 11 times.

So, when it comes right down to it, there really isn't an old new-shoe tradition at all. But a few finance ministers who thought there was came up with their own personal approaches to the idea. In December 1979 minister of finance John Crosbie strode into the House of Commons to deliver his budget speech wearing a pair of mukluks, and in February 1994 Paul Martin wore a new pair of work boots. And for his March 2007 budget Jim Flaherty didn't buy new shoes for himself; instead, he bought a new pair of skates for his son.

What's that, eh?

If you hear the word snotty on Prince Edward Island, it might not mean what you think if you assume it's referring to a snobbish person or to the face of a little kid with a runny nose. An Islander might very well use snotty to describe a damp, grey day with a light rain falling. That's snotty weather on P.E.I.

DID YOU KNOW...

...that Gimli, Manitoba, on the southwestern shore of Lake Winnipeg, is home to the world's largest number of people of Icelandic descent outside Iceland itself? Immigrants from Iceland looking for a better life first began settling there in 1875, and the community has maintained a distinctive Icelandic culture to this day. The ever-popular Icelandic Festival of Manitoba has been held there in early August every year since 1932.

A Canadian Viking

In 1967 Gimli, Manitoba, chose to celebrate Canada's centennial — the country's hundredth birthday — by having a really big statue built. In keeping with its Icelandic roots, the town erected a 4.6-metre-high fibreglass Viking!

Thinking Big for the Fun of It

In the early 1990s Gladstone, Manitoba, about 150 kilometres west of Gimli, decided it wanted a big roadside attraction too, one that would welcome tourists travelling along the Yellowhead Trans-Canada Highway. In 1993, with a wink and a nod to the town's name, an 11-metre-high monument was built, topped by a huge, round, smiling fellow. His name? Happy Rock, of course. And to encourage travellers to drop in for a visit, the good people of Gladstone spread the word that it was good luck to get your picture taken under the statue of Happy Rock. Clever folks, those Gladstone residents, and with a sense of humour too.

Have Rock, Will Travel

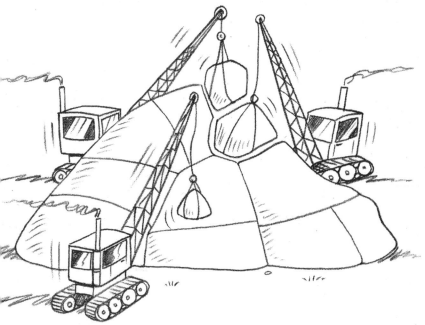

The Happy Rock monument in Gladstone is made of
fibreglass and weighs about 1.4 tonnes. In the 1990s
designers of a small park in Yorkville, Toronto's most
fashionable shopping and dining district, also wanted a
big rock to welcome tourists. But they wanted the real
thing — a one-billion-year-old piece of granite that was
located about 180 kilometres north of the city, and
which weighed in at a whopping 650 tonnes.

Getting that rock to Toronto was a major challenge. First the top 2.1 metres of a massive area of weather-worn Canadian Shield granite had to be sliced off — in 135 manageable pieces weighing from about 225 to 900 kilograms. Each piece was labelled to show how it fitted with the others, and then a crane loaded the sections onto 20 flatbed trucks for the trip south. When the pieces arrived in Toronto, cranes unloaded them and workers guided them into their correct positions at the park site, wedging them together like pieces of a giant jigsaw puzzle. Then the joints were heat-sealed together to make the 19-metre by 15-metre rock's surface look like one solid piece again. Voilà! A bit of natural landscape transplanted to a bustling city street ...

DID YOU KNOW...

...that the first park in the world north of the Arctic Circle was Auyuittuq National Park on Nunavut's Baffin Island? There's no need to move any rocks to this vast park. It consists of nearly 20 000 square kilometres of towering granite mountains, up to 300-metre-deep ice fields and 900-metre-high coastal cliffs, or fjords. The park was established in 1976. Its name, Auyuittuq, is an Inuktitut word that means "land that never melts."

A Real Cutie

Melody and Carl-Richard Dancel, from Tecumseh, Ontario, thought their eight-month-old daughter, Cameron, was as cute as a button. But they had no idea she'd be considered contest-winning cute. However, Melody figured she had nothing to lose by entering a photo of their little girl in a "Beautiful Baby Search" competition being run by the *Live with Regis and Kelly* morning television show. On February 5, 2007, about an hour and a half before the contest's website stopped accepting entries, she posted a favourite picture of Cameron on-line, unaware that at least 150 000 other proud parents had entered photos too.

But a few weeks later, Melody ended up being the proudest and most excited parent of them all. She, her daughter and her husband were flown to New York City to appear live on the show — because Cameron had won the contest. Her prize? Her photo on the cover of the Summer 2007 issue of *Parenting* magazine, and $5000 toward her college education. Emily Saniga, a toddler from Toronto, Ontario, was another winner, receiving $1000 for placing fifth in the competition.

Debby Hits Forty — Party On!

In December 2006 a polar bear named Debby, one of the most popular residents of Winnipeg, Manitoba, turned forty. Orphaned soon after she was born in the Russian Arctic and unable to survive on her own, Debby was just a few months old when she was sent to Winnipeg in the spring of 1967. She settled in to her new home at the Assiniboine Park Zoo and quickly became a hit with visitors. She grew up and met her mate, Skipper, there, and over the years the contented couple had six healthy baby bears. Skipper was 34 when he died in 2001, an unusually old age for a polar bear, but not nearly as unusual as

Debby's. The average life span of a polar bear is about 15 years, and it's rare for one to make it past 20.

After Debby's 40th birthday, 17-year-old Samantha Machan decided to send news of that special event to Guinness World Records, and in August 2007, Machan and zoo officials learned that Debby had made it into the record book as the world's oldest living polar bear. Debby took the news in stride, doing what she usually did each day — curling up for a long nap.

He said What?

"*If you don't protect your cabin or your house, you will have to redecorate.*"
— Reg Bell, elementary school student,
Churchill, Manitoba

Reg was referring to the mess a polar bear can make if it manages to break into a building in Churchill.

A Bear-y
Safe Halloween

In Churchill, Manitoba, more than 1000 kilometres north of Winnipeg, people don't have to go to the zoo to see polar bears. In the fall the bears often wander into town looking for a snack. The males drop in on their way to the ice floes on Hudson Bay where they'll find plenty of seals to eat, and the females check out the place on their way to dens about 150 kilometres south where they'll give birth.

Tourists from around the world travel to Churchill for a chance to watch these magnificent creatures, but the last thing local parents want to see lumbering through town when their children are outside is a big, powerful, hungry polar bear. And Halloween is one day when kids definitely want to be out and about, even in the polar bear capital of the world. So, to make sure they can go trick-or-treating like other kids across the country, the town's polar bear patrol goes into action.

Starting on October 30, police, parks officials, firefighters, paramedics and volunteers make regular rounds of the town looking for bears. If they spot one, they try to scare it off with sirens and bright lights, but if that doesn't work, they shoot it with a tranquilizer gun. When it's sound asleep, they move it to a compound known as the polar bear jail until a helicopter can fly it far away from Churchill.

And when it comes to choosing a costume, dressing all in white is a definite no-no. You do not want to be mistaken for a bear that gets targeted with a tranquilizer dart. Wearing a seal costume isn't such a good idea either. If a hungry bear did manage to get past the patrols, it might find a young seal look-alike very tempting.

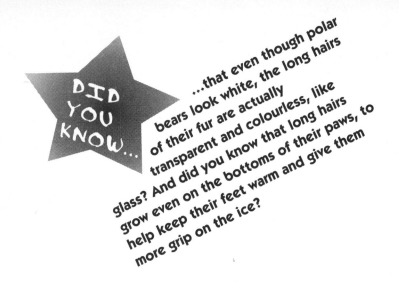

Bigfoot Believer?
Or Not?

On April 4, 2007, Mike Lake, Conservative Member of Parliament for the Edmonton-Mill Woods riding in Alberta, said that he didn't make judgment calls on petitions submitted to him by his constituents. But maybe he should have before agreeing to present one particular petition in the House of Commons on March 28, 2007. It asked the federal government to legally protect none other than the big, hairy beast known as Bigfoot — by granting it endangered species status.

Some people wondered aloud why a creature whose existence is questionable would need to be protected

from becoming endangered. Others asked why Lake would waste Parliament's time with such an issue when there were more important things for it — and him — to worry about. When questioned, Lake said he didn't personally support the petition, because he didn't believe Bigfoot existed.

Prime Minister Harper's government had 45 days in which to respond. Lake probably breathed a sigh of relief when the government let the deadline pass without taking any action.

Banking on
the Future

When award-winning actor and comedian Jim Carrey was just a kid growing up in Newmarket, Ontario, he was already making his friends laugh with his jokes and silly routines. They thought he was really funny, and he did too, so when he was only 10 he dared to mail in an application to work on *The Carol Burnett Show*, a popular comedy hour on TV in the early 1970s.

Not surprisingly, Carrey didn't get the job, but he didn't get discouraged either. As an older teen, he was still so confident he'd make it in the entertainment business that he wrote himself a postdated cheque for $10 million, vowing to carry it around in his wallet until he had earned that much money.

Carrey moved to Los Angeles, California, in the early 1980s and after a lot of hard work he did make it big, doing so well as a comic and an actor that by late 1995, the date he had written on that cheque years earlier, he was actually worth $10 million. And by 1996 he was doing so very well that he was paid twice that much to star in just one film, *The Cable Guy*.

He said What?

"You miss one hundred per cent of the shots you never take."
— Wayne Gretzky, hockey superstar

DID YOU KNOW...

...that in the entertaining family film *MVP: Most Valuable Primate*, Jack, the stick-handling chimpanzee star, plays hockey for the fictional Nelson Nuggets of Nelson, British Columbia?

The movie was filmed at several locations in B.C. — at the VIA Rail station, GM Place, the Kerrisdale Arena and the University of British Columbia's Thunderbird Arena (all in Vancouver); in Squamish; and at Vancouver International Airport on Sea Island in Richmond.

The Most Valuable Player in Manitoba

On March 18, 2005, 66-year-old Phyllis Thomas of Peguis, Manitoba, stopped on her way to Winnipeg to watch a grandson play hockey and bought two lottery tickets. Later that evening, she scratched off the coating to reveal the numbers, and was amazed to discover that one ticket was a really big winner worth $1 million.

Two years later, on March 31, 2007, Thomas stopped on her way to Winnipeg to watch a grandson play hockey and bought two lottery tickets. Later that evening, she scratched off the coating to reveal the numbers, and was absolutely stunned to discover that she held another really big winning ticket — another one worth $1 million!

What Time Is It, Anyway?

Canada is so wide that it's divided into six time zones: Pacific, Mountain, Central, Eastern, Atlantic and Newfoundland Standard Time. So there's a 4-hour time difference between places in British Columbia and Newfoundland.

As well, each spring Canada switches to daylight saving time, which is one hour later than standard time. Since 2007 the switch happens on the second Sunday of March — and the country returns to using standard time on the first weekend of November.

So if you know about the time zones and daylight saving time, you shouldn't have any trouble figuring out what time it is. But ...

... Saskatchewan doesn't switch to daylight saving time in the spring. Except for Denare Beach, Sturgeon Landing and Creighton, Saskatchewan, which do switch because folks there want to run on the same time as Flin Flon, Manitoba, during the summer months. Lloydminster, which is right on the Saskatchewan-Alberta border, switches too. And ...

... Dawson Creek and Fort St. John in British Columbia stay on Mountain Standard Time all year long. That means they're actually on Pacific Standard Time during the summer when British Columbia switches to daylight saving time. And ...

... Atikokan, Ontario, because it's west of the 90°W line of longitude, is supposed to keep Central Standard Time, but it stays on Eastern Standard Time all year long. That means in the winter it's using the same time as Thunder Bay, Ontario, and in the summer it's on the same time as Fort Frances and Rainy River when they're on Central Daylight Saving Time. And ...

... with few exceptions, all places in Quebec east of the 63°W line of longitude are on Atlantic Standard Time, and all those west of that are on Eastern Standard Time. And ...

... there are several more exceptions — which makes keeping track of keeping time in Canada sound very complicated. In most cases it's not, but probably the best answer to the question, "What time is it?" is, "It all depends on where you are."

Making Sure Everyone's On Time

Canada's provinces and territories all have laws that regulate what time it's supposed to be in each of their regions of the country. But some cities and towns, such as Atikokan, Ontario, most parts of Labrador, and Creighton, Saskatchewan, simply ignore those laws because they think life is easier if their residents are using the same time as nearby communities with which they are in regular contact.

Many people living in Moosomin, Saskatchewan, work just across the border in Manitoba. They wish their town would switch to daylight saving time every spring,

IT'S LATER THAN YOU THINK IN SASKATCHEWAN, IF IT'S NOT REALLY AS EARLY AS YOU THINK IT IS IN MANITOBA!

IT'S STILL BEDTIME!

even though it's not supposed to. From spring to late fall, when the clock says 7 a.m. in their town, it says 8 a.m. in Manitoba. So while their neighbours who work in Saskatchewan are still sleeping, they're hustling to get to work!

Determined to make sure everyone in Alberta switched to daylight saving time each spring, that province's government actually passed a law in 2000 saying that "no person shall . . . use or observe within Alberta any time other than Daylight Saving Time," and that any person who doesn't "is guilty of an offence and liable to a fine not exceeding $25." One can't help wondering how officials would know if a person wasn't operating on daylight saving time. And if they did find some persons who weren't, would they keep fining them $25 over and over again if they refused to set their clocks forward an hour? Hmm ...

They said What?

"*Would it be fair not to give the fans the chance to see my beautiful face?*"

— Lorne "Gump" Worsley

Montreal-born Worsley was a hockey Hall-of-Famer who was a goalie in the NHL from 1953 to 1974. He played a total of 861 games, and only wore a mask for the last six of them.

"I already had four broken noses, a broken jaw, two broken cheekbones, and almost 200 stitches in my head. I didn't care how the mask looked. I was afraid I would look just like the mask, the way things were going."
— Jacques Plante

Plante, of Shawinigan Falls, Quebec, was an all-star NHL goalie who played at the same time as Worsley. Plante began wearing a full face mask in 1959. He was the first NHL goalie to do so full-time.

Canada's Four Corners

A quadripoint is a point on the earth that touches four distinctly separate regions of the world. A secondary quadripoint is a point where the boundaries of four political subdivisions, such as provinces or states, meet. There aren't very many quadripoints in the world, but there is one in Canada. It's located in the far north, at the southeastern end of Lake Kasba, which is mainly in the Northwest Territories. There the boundaries of Saskatchewan, Manitoba, the Northwest Territories and Nunavut meet at a point, like a four-corner intersection or crossing.

...that Quebec is the only province that borders three other provinces? It touches both New Brunswick and Newfoundland and Labrador on the east, and it borders Ontario on the west.

Oops!
Wrong Direction!

Many Canadians make the mistake of thinking that if they want to go from Windsor, Ontario, to Detroit, Michigan, they have to head south. But Windsor, located at 42º18' N, is *south* of Detroit at 42º23' N. Check it out on a map.

The Western Giant

That's the nickname given to 1.94-metre-tall John "Jack" Hugh Gillis, who was finally inducted into British Columbia's Sports Hall of Fame in 2006 — 100 years after he arrived in Vancouver.

Soon after he settled there in 1906, Gillis joined the Vancouver Police Force. He also started entering — and winning — "All-Round" competitions, a combination of several track and field events a lot like decathlons today.

In 1909 he became the All-Round Champion of Canada, and the next year he placed second in the American All-Round Championship. As the holder of more than 60 medals in various events, he was really looking forward to doing well at the 1912 Olympics in Stockholm, Sweden, but was terribly disappointed when he fell ill and couldn't go. A year later, when he was just 29, he died, a victim of tuberculosis.

One of Gillis's shotput throws was so long it set a record that stood for 32 years. But Gillis, originally from Cape Breton, Nova Scotia, held another record that was even more impressive. It had to do with how he got to British Columbia. On February 3, 1906 — long before a network of roads connected east to west — he set out on foot from Sydney, Nova Scotia. He arrived in Vancouver nearly eight months later, on September 24. Gillis followed the train tracks whenever he could, but he didn't ride the rails. Instead, he became the first person ever to walk across Canada.

Just
the
Stats

In the summer of 2005, Canadians took 12.2 million trips to go swimming, 8.2 million trips to go boating and 6.4 million trips to go fishing. Canadians also spent $1.5 billion on plants for their gardens, buying nearly 570 million flowers and 465 million vegetables.

Playgrounds for All

Many Canadian families can't afford to head to the lake each summer to go swimming and boating, but the fun that kids can have on public playgrounds in every city and town across the country is free, thanks in part to the efforts of a New Brunswicker named Mabel Phoebe Peters.

Peters was born in Saint John, New Brunswick, in 1861. Her father ran a hotel there, and in the late 1800s she and her sister helped him run it. Peters was also very active in the early women's rights movement, and a strong believer in a community's responsibility to help families care for their children.

Seeing kids playing in the streets and getting into all sorts of mischief during summer holidays, she began a campaign in the early 1900s to get local councils to set up safe, publicly funded play areas.

In 1906, with help from a local newspaper editor, she gathered enough local support and donations to set up the Allison Ground Playground in Saint John, the first public playground in Canada. She then spent the next few years before her death in 1914 travelling to many Canadian cities, promoting the creation of playgrounds for all. It's still a great idea.

DID YOU KNOW...

...that the wettest city in Canada is Prince Rupert, British Columbia, with an average of just over 2590 millimetres of precipitation a year? Prince Rupert is also the cloudiest city, putting up with about 6150 hours of grey, overcast skies each year. But Prince Rupert faces its shortage of dry, sunny days head on, proudly assuming the title of Cloudiest and Wettest City in Canada.

Cold Summer – 1999

Prince Rupert residents may take their damp, grey days in stride, but folks in Calgary, Alberta, complained loudly about the summer of 1999. It wasn't just mainly damp and grey; it was also miserably cold. More snow fell in Calgary in July of that year than in February. On July 15 the daytime temperature plummeted to 2.7°C. With winds gusting to more than 50 kilometres per hour that day, it felt like -14°C at times — definitely not shorts weather.

She said What?

" 'Snow in April is abominable,' said Anne. 'Like a slap in the face when you expected a kiss.' "
— Lucy Maud Montgomery

The "Anne" in this quote is Anne Shirley, the unforgettable fictional character brought to life by Canadian author Lucy Maud Montgomery in *Anne of Green Gables*, published in 1908. Since then millions of readers around the world have fallen in love with Anne, and with her home province of Prince Edward Island.

Surely Anne would have sympathized with Calgarians during the summer of 1999. One can only imagine what words she would have used to describe snow in July — "devastating"? "unbearable"? Or perhaps she would have found such a possibility "utterly unspeakable" . . .

Warm Summer - 1999

But while Calgarians shivered in the west, many Newfoundlanders in the east enjoyed warmer-than-usual summer weather in 1999. It was so warm that, for only the second time in nearly a century, not a single iceberg drifted south of St. John's. They had all melted. Some years up to 1000 icebergs have made it that far south.

Bidding Harry a Fond Farewell

In early August 2007, just a few weeks after *Harry Potter and the Deathly Hallows* hit the bookstores, Toronto, Ontario, played host to the world's largest Harry Potter conference, Prophecy 2007.

About 1500 fans and scholars from around the world — no one under 14 allowed — gathered in the Sheraton Centre downtown for four days of lectures, discussions, film screenings, quidditch games, wizardry duels, costume balls and quiet time spent in the Hall of Reflection, looking fondly back on a ten-year-long journey spent with Harry and sadly remembering beloved characters who died along the way.

A magically fantastic time was had by all. Long live Harry Potter!

Live Long and Prosper:
Greetings from Vulcan

Vulcan, Alberta, about 130 kilometres southeast of Calgary, was originally named in the early 1900s after the Roman god of fire. But the name took on an added dimension with the phenomenal success of the *Star Trek* television series and films that featured pointy-eared aliens like Spock, Sarek and Tuvok from the planet Vulcan. Hoping to attract more tourists to their town, some real-life Vulcans decided to have a local welder named Gary McKinnon build a really big spaceship that looked very much like the TV show's famed starship, the USS *Enterprise*.

McKinnon finished the nearly 9.5-metre-long ship in June 1995. Impressive enough in the daytime, it's even more alluring at night when it's lit in such a way that it appears to be hovering above the ground at the entrance to the town. In the fall of 1998, the town added a 16-metre-tall space station that serves as the area's tourism centre and also features science fact-and-fiction displays of interest to visitors, especially Trekkies — extremely loyal *Star Trek* fans.

And Trekkies do make their way to Vulcan; in fact, hundreds of them, complete with costumes, turn up each year when the town plays host to the Spock Days/Galaxyfest convention. In 2007 Vulcan added a popular new attraction in keeping with the Star Trek theme — a virtual reality game that lets players stand on the bridge of a starship and defend it from alien invaders (not Vulcans, of course).

Putting Out the Welcome Mat for UFOs

The *Enterprise* look-alike starship "landed" in Vulcan, Alberta, on schedule in 1995. But about 600 kilometres north, people in St. Paul, Alberta, have been waiting since 1967 for a spaceship to land there.

Taking a lighthearted approach to choosing a Centennial project celebrating Canada's 100th birthday, some residents decided to show that St. Paul was such a visitor-friendly place it would even welcome travellers aboard UFOs — unidentified flying objects. So they had the world's first UFO landing pad — 12 metres wide — built right in the middle of town. Beside the pad they erected a sign with the following message:

> REPUBLIC OF ST. PAUL
> (STARGATE ALPHA)
> THE AREA UNDER THE WORLD'S FIRST UFO LANDING PAD WAS DESIGNATED INTERNATIONAL BY THE TOWN OF ST. PAUL AS A SYMBOL OF OUR FAITH THAT MANKIND WILL MAINTAIN THE OUTER UNIVERSE FREE FROM NATIONAL WARS AND STRIFE. THAT FUTURE TRAVEL IN SPACE WILL BE SAFE FOR ALL INTERGALACTIC BEINGS. ALL VISITORS FROM EARTH OR OTHERWISE ARE WELCOME TO THIS TERRITORY AND TO THE TOWN OF ST. PAUL.

Over the years UFOs seemed to have trouble locating St. Paul, though the landing pad did start luring a few more visitors off the highway. But the numbers zoomed up in 1995 after the local Chamber of Commerce decided, just for the fun of it, to set up a 1-800 hotline number that people could call to report UFO sightings. Much to their surprise, the calls started coming in by the thousands, and not just to report seeing mysterious flying objects. People called about being abducted by aliens, about seeing spooky lights, and about finding bizarre crop circles, or cattle cut up and studied by aliens, in their fields.

The publicity possibilities were irresistible. In 1998 St. Paul decided to hold an international UFO conference, and 200 delegates came. They hosted another one two years later, and about 600 people came!

The wacky idea of building the big pad back in 1967 was finally paying off. Fans of aliens, if not aliens themselves, were landing in St. Paul, and residents welcomed them — and their tourist dollars — with open arms.

Just the Stats

According to the 2006 Canadian UFO Survey, 736 UFO sightings were reported to UFOlogy Research of Manitoba that year. About 650 of those strange apparitions turned out to be identifiable things such as planes, planets, and meteors, leaving about 85 sightings that couldn't be explained away so easily . . .

What ELSE Is Out There?

Actor James Doohan was born in Vancouver, British Columbia, and moved to Sarnia, Ontario, as a teenager. When he was just 19, he enlisted in the Canadian army, and was hit six times by machine gun fire during the D-Day invasion of Normandy. After recovering from his wounds, he learned to fly and served as an army pilot until the end of the Second World War.

After the war, Doohan became an actor, and it was in his fictional role as an officer aboard something much bigger than an airplane that he became a star on the hit TV series, *Star Trek*. Doohan played the part of Montgomery Scott, the inventive space engineer who kept the massive starship *Enterprise* running and regularly obeyed Captain Kirk's command to "Beam me up, Scotty." His Scotty character was such a hit with fans that many teenagers gave him credit for inspiring them to become engineers.

Doohan died at age 85 in 2005. Two years later his family honoured a request he had made in his will, and beamed him up into the sky. On April 28, 2007, aboard a rocket operated by a private company in Houston, Texas, some of Doohan's cremated remains were launched into space, a fitting final real-life journey for one who had so often boldly gone, in a fictional world, where no man had gone before.

...that in terms of the value of the diamonds mined, Canada is the third largest diamond producer in the world? The first Canadian diamonds were found around Lac de Gras in the Northwest Territories in 1991. As of 2007 there were three diamond mines operating in the NWT and a fourth one in Nunavut.

Canadian Pizza Company Delivers — to Afghanistan!

In the fall of 2003 Corporal Patrick Cyr was serving with Canadian forces stationed in Kabul, Afghanistan. He kept in touch with his family back in Canada via e-mails. In one e-mail to his brother, Michael, he mentioned that one of the things he missed was a good pizza. Reading that, Michael decided to send some pizza to his brother — and about 2000 other soldiers at the same camp.

As executive vice-president of Boston Pizza International, Michael had no problem getting people at

his company excited about his plan. The firm's president, Michael Cordoba, loved the idea, seeing it as a great way to show support for members of Canada's armed forces. Company officials contacted military officials and arrangements were made to include a container loaded with pizza fixings on a transport plane leaving the Canadian Forces base in Trenton, Ontario, on October 31.

Two days later 2200 frozen pizza shells and all the sauce, cheese and toppings needed to dress them arrived in Kabul. On November 11 — Remembrance Day — kitchen staff at the base made and cooked the pizzas and "delivered" them to Patrick Cyr and his fellow soldiers, compliments of his brother and everyone else at Boston Pizza back in Canada, more than 10 500 kilometres away.

The Biggest Coin
in the World

Speaking of pizzas, in early May 2007, the Royal Canadian Mint in Ottawa introduced a new maple leaf coin about the size of an extra-large pizza. The colossal coin, 53 centimetres across and more than 3 centimetres thick, isn't just too big to slip into a pocket; it's also too heavy, weighing in at a whopping 100 kilograms. And since it's made of 99.99 per cent pure gold, it's also a bit too expensive for most collectors to add to their Christmas gift wish list. The face value of the coin is $1 million, but the actual price one would have to pay is at least $2 million, based on the going rate for 28.35 grams (one ounce) of gold.

She said What?

"*They told me I was going to have the tallest, darkest leading man in Hollywood. Naturally I thought of Clark Gable.*"

— Fay Wray

Actress Fay Wray, born in Cardston, Alberta, in 1907, said this when talking about being offered the leading lady role in the 1933 film classic, *King Kong*. Her dreamy leading man turned out to be a tall, dark, giant gorilla!

A Smash Hit

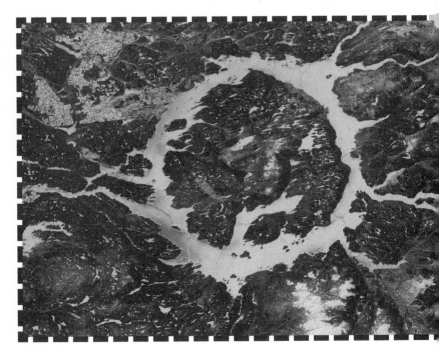

It's sometimes called "the eye of Quebec," and rightly so, because when seen from high above Earth, that's exactly what it looks like — a giant eye.

This amazing geological formation is the result of an event that happened more than 200 million years ago when a huge asteroid from outer space smashed into the rocky Canadian Shield of northern Quebec. When the asteroid hit, it sent intense shock waves through the rock, shooting broken pieces outward from the impact zone and leaving behind a massive crater about

100 kilometres across. Over millions of years the movement of glacial ice across the area scraped away the broken rock, scouring out a rim that filled with melting ice, creating an annular, or ring-shaped, lake called Lake Manicouagan. Like the white of an eye around the dark iris and pupil, the lake surrounds a large island — René-Levasseur Island.

Over a very long time erosion has shrunk the crater, known as the Manicouagan impact crater, but it's still 65 kilometres across, making it one of the five largest known impact craters on Earth. It so impressed astronaut Marc Garneau when he saw it from space that he nominated it for the Seven Wonders of Canada when the Canadian Broadcasting Corporation ran a competition asking Canadians to submit their choices.

And the Winners Were . . .

In 2007 tens of thousands of Canadians submitted dozens of selections, and the popularity of their choices helped the judges come up with the final list of Seven Wonders of Canada — a list that reflects both the natural and human history of the country.

Niagara Falls
The Rocky Mountains
The Prairie Skies
Old Quebec City

Pier 21 in Halifax
The Igloo
The Canoe

Paddling Through History

Not everyone agreed with the results of the CBC's competition, but some folks at a museum in Peterborough, Ontario, were delighted to hear of one of the judges' seven choices.

From 1850 to 1960 several famous canoe factories were located in Peterborough, making it the world's centre for canoe building, and in 1997 the city also became home to The Canadian Canoe Museum, the largest canoe museum in the world. Its collection includes more than 600 canoes and kayaks of all shapes and sizes, as well as many other items associated with the history and uses of these lightweight boats so well suited to travel along Canada's vast network of waterways.

First Nations and Inuit people, whose ancestors were the original designers of these crafts, the many dedicated people who run and support the museum, and the museum's founder, University of Toronto professor Kirk Wipper, would all agree that the canoe deserves its place on the list of the Seven Wonders of Canada. So do millions of other Canadians.

There are more than 2.4 million paddlers — both canoeists and kayakers — in Canada.

A BIG Red Paper Clip

In 2006 Kipling, a town of about 1000 in southeastern Saskatchewan, installed something new in Bell Park — a 4.6-metre-long steel paper clip. It's painted bright red and it's strong enough for kids to climb all over if they want to, but that's not the main reason it was erected in Kipling. It may not be big enough to make it into the record books as the world's biggest paper clip, but it might be big enough to attract more visitors to town, especially during the annual Red Paper Clip Festival held in July.

The REAL Red Paper Clip

It's hard to imagine why people would want to stop by to see a paper clip, even if it is a big one. But Kipling's connection with a real paper clip turned out to be a publicity dream come true.

On July 12, 2005, Montrealer Kyle MacDonald posted his willingness to trade a small red paper clip on an Internet site, hoping he would receive something better. Sure enough, someone offered him a fish-shaped pen and he made the trade. Then he offered to trade the pen, and accepted an E.T.-shaped doorknob (of *E.T.: The Extra-Terrestrial* film fame). He traded the doorknob for a Coleman stove, the stove for a gas-powered generator, the generator for a keg of beer and

beer party, the beer for a snowmobile, the snowmobile for a trip to Yahk, British Columbia, the trip for a 1995 cube van, the van for a recording contract, the contract for a rent-free apartment in Phoenix, Arizona, for a year, and the apartment for an afternoon with rocker Alice Cooper.

By then MacDonald's trading had attracted a lot of publicity both on-line and on TV and radio, and the millions of people following his story were really surprised when he traded away the afternoon with Cooper for a KISS (an American rock band) snow globe. However, one of the people who had heard about MacDonald's activities was actor and independent filmmaker Corbin Bernsen. He had offered MacDonald a part in a film as a possible trade item. MacDonald figured he should try to get something Bernsen would really like to have in return. He found out that Bernsen was a keen snow globe collector so he had deliberately traded "down" to the snow globe.

MacDonald got the movie role, and then offered to trade it, and that's when Kipling, Saskatchewan, came into the picture. The town offered MacDonald a house on Main Street in exchange for the movie role. MacDonald accepted — and in 2006 he and his wife moved there. Thanks to all the publicity he had received, MacDonald got a book contract and a film deal too.

The town held local auditions for the movie role. Corbin Bernsen showed up and gave 19-year-old Nolan Hubbard from Kipling a part in his film, *Donna on Demand*. Bernson also started making plans to film his next movie, *3 Day Test,* in Kipling, and to use several local people in it.

So, in the end, MacDonald traded a small, red plastic paper clip for a house, and Kipling, Saskatchewan, got a big, red steel one that kids can climb on.

Multi-Million-Dollar Penguins

Lane Merrifield, Dave Krysko and Lance Priebe, three dads from Kelowna, British Columbia, figured one way to make sure preteens could have a safe place to "hang out" on the Internet was to design one themselves. So, in 2005, they launched a subscription website called Club Penguin, populated by lovable virtual penguins whose activities encouraged kids to have fun and be creative in an ad-free space.

The founders' timing couldn't have been better. Two very successful films about penguins were released around the same time — *March of the Penguins* in 2005, and *Happy Feet* in 2006. The club proved to be such a hit that by 2007 it had 700 000 paying "members" worldwide, and the company was employing a staff of 100 in Kelowna. Wealthy investors began to make offers to buy the company, but it wasn't until one promised to keep Club Penguin ad-free and leave its headquarters in Kelowna that the three founders decided to sell. The buyer? The Walt Disney Company! And the selling price? A cool $350 million, with a promise of up to $350 million more by the end of 2009 if the number of subscriptions kept growing as predicted.

Multi-Million-Dollar Shoes

Another British Columbia parent, Sandra Wilson, wanted to find some comfortable shoes that would stay on her 18-month-old son's chubby little feet. She also wanted to find work that would let her spend as much time as possible with young Robert when her maternity leave ended. So she came up with a plan to design soft-soled leather booties — the kind of shoes she wished she could find for Robert — and to start working at home in North Vancouver making lots of them to sell to other parents.

Her plan worked, her designs were great, and to make a long success story short, Robeez Footwear Limited — the home-based company she started in 1994 — became so successful that by 2006 it had sales topping $15 million and employed nearly 400 workers. On September 6, 2007, Wilson agreed to sell her company to a major American shoe retailer, The Stride Rite Corporation, for $30.5 million. On the same day that she said goodbye to Robeez Footwear, she waved goodbye to her son Robert as he headed off to his first day at high school — 13 years after she had named her company after him.

He said What?

"The only time money is important is when you haven't any."
— Max Bell

Albertan George Maxwell Bell was a successful businessman, newspaper publisher and owner of many winning thoroughbred horses. He was also a generous philanthropist, donating a lot of money to many good causes. In 1977, five years after his death, Bell was named to the Canadian Horse Racing Hall of Fame.

They're at the post!
They're off!
She wins!

On September 14, 2001, Emma-Jayne Wilson wrote on a piece of paper, "I, Emma-Jayne Wilson, promise — promise — to make it as a jockey." Nearly six years later, on June 24, 2007, the 148th running of the Queen's Plate took place at Woodbine racetrack in

Toronto, Ontario. One of the horses running in that race was Mike Fox, and the jockey riding him was Emma-Jayne Wilson. Mike Fox came from behind in the last 70 or so metres to win Canada's most important race for thoroughbreds, and Wilson made horse-racing history, becoming the first female jockey to ride a Queen's Plate winner across the finish line.

DID YOU KNOW...

...that Bob Hope, the legendary American comedian and actor after whom a major golf tournament is named, played his very first game of golf in Winnipeg, Manitoba, in 1930?

During breaks from participating in a variety show running at a theatre there, Hope joined some fellow performers who were spending their spare time golfing at a local course, and teed off for the very first time.

Students Outsmart Smarties' Maker

In the fall of 2005 Tanja Coghill, a teacher in Thunder Bay, Ontario, noticed that one fun fact printed on a box of Smarties claimed that Canadians ate four billion Smarties a year — enough Smarties to encircle the world 350 times. Coghill decided that checking that fact would be a great math assignment for her Grade 6 students.

The students measured the sugar-coated chocolate candies made by Nestlé and learned that the diameter of each was one centimetre. That meant that four billion of them laid end to end would be four billion centimetres — or 40 000 kilometres — long. But when they found out that the circumference of Earth is about 40 000 kilometres, they realized something was wrong with the fact printed on the box. If the four billion number was right, Canadians ate enough Smarties each year to encircle the world just once, not 350 times. And if the 350 times number was right, Canadians would have to eat one trillion four hundred billion Smarties a year!

Either way, the students figured out that the information on the candy box needed revising. They wrote three letters to the Nestlé company pointing out the error before they got an answer back telling them that in 2006 it would be dropped from the Smarties packages sold in Canada.

"If you're not annoying somebody, you're not really alive."
— Margaret Atwood

Margaret Atwood was born in Ottawa, Ontario, in 1939, and grew up in northern Ontario and Quebec. An internationally renowned, award-winning author and poet, she's also been an outspoken supporter of many worthwhile causes.

...that the section of Ontario's Highway 401 which runs through Toronto is the busiest stretch of road in North America?

Also known as the MacDonald-Cartier Freeway, the major transportation artery stretches nearly 820 kilometres east from Windsor, Ontario, to the Ontario-Quebec border, most of it as a four-lane divided highway. But in the Toronto area the roadway is 12 to 20 lanes wide in some places and carries more than 400 000 vehicles a day.

Just the Stats

Between 2001 and 2006 the Royal Canadian Mounted Police force spent an average of $11.6 million a year on uniforms. There are 121 items included in the outfit needed to dress each officer, including four different types of hats, seven different kinds of footwear and six types of coats or jackets. And since 2001, even though most Mounties don't ride horses any more, the force has bought nearly $400 000 worth of spurs.

Monster Tooth

When nine-year-old Mark Henry of Francis Lake, Ontario, left the dentist's office one day in 2005, he had lost a tooth and gained a world record. The incisor the dentist had to pull to make room for another tooth trying to grow in Mark's mouth turned out to be super huge, as human teeth go. It was a whopping 2.28 centimetres long and 1.2 centimetres wide, the largest human tooth on record.

Gopher Problems

The small town of Torrington, Alberta, about 120 kilometres north of Calgary, has had a gopher problem for a long time. The gophers (actually Richardson's ground squirrels) are furry brown rodents about 30 centimetres long. They burrow extensive tunnels, leaving behind mounds of dirt and holes that can break the legs of cows. They're also hungry little vegetarians, dining on field crops and vegetable gardens, munching up to 60 per cent of their body weight every day. So farmers in the area feel they have to keep the gopher population under control. That means killing some of them.

When the Alberta government started a grant program in 1995 to help small towns come up with ways to attract more people, Torrington decided to look on the bright side of its gopher problem and apply for money to set up the world's first gopher museum. The grant money came through and the Torrington Gopher Hole Museum opened in June 1996 — to a flurry of controversy.

The museum displays six dozen stuffed (by a taxidermist) gophers dressed in detailed costumes and posed to look like the types of people you might find living and working in and around the town. When some animal rights groups heard about the museum's "residents" they began a campaign to stop people from visiting, saying displaying animals this way disrespects them, even if they are dead.

Various papers and magazines ran stories about the controversy, and letters of complaint arrived at the museum from as far away as Germany, England and Japan.

But letters of support started coming too, and to the amazement of the 200 or so human residents of Torrington, so did visitors — several thousand a year since the tiny one-room museum opened in 1996!

The Case of
the Missing Cheese

In October 2004 La Fromagerie Boivin, a cheese-making company in La Baie, Quebec, dropped 10 barrels of aging cheddar into the very deep, chilly waters of the Saguenay Fjord, near Tadoussac, Quebec. Luc Boivin, the firm's vice-president, decided to submerge the 800 kilograms of cheese, worth more than $40 000, in the hope that it would develop a tasty new flavour ripening under the high pressure exerted by the water.

But when Boivin came back in the summer of 2005 to pull up the cheese, he couldn't find it. After spending nearly $40 000 hiring divers with high-tech equipment to look for the sunken cheese, Boivin finally gave up the search. Did strong currents send the anchored barrels down the Saguenay River into the St. Lawrence? Did some lucky people fishing in the area snag a barrel and secretly return to make off with the rest? Or is the cheese still hiding deep in the fjord, ripening into the tastiest cheese ever made? The mystery of the missing cheese is a cold case, still waiting to be solved.

What's that, eh?

Skunky is a Canadian adjective used mainly to describe beer that's gone "off" and that tastes and smells foul. The word skunk itself comes from an Abenaki First Nation word *segongw*. The word moose is also Abenaki in origin, coming from the word *mos*.

Just the Stats

A 2.4-kilogram chicken produces about 100 grams of manure a day. A 195-kilogram pig eliminates just under 20 kilograms daily and a milk-producing cow weighing about 625 kilograms produces about 69 kilograms a day. That's a lot of poop! Fortunately, it can be recycled as fertilizer.

More Stats

In 2006 Canadian hens produced 588.4 million dozens of eggs. Canadians eat an average of 150 eggs per year.

Spuds Rule

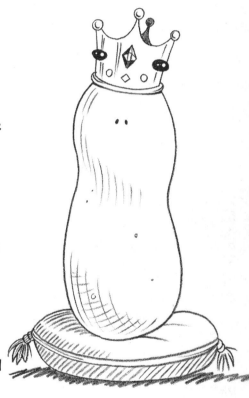

The rich red soil of Prince Edward Island is ideally suited to the growing of potatoes. Farmers have been growing them there since 1790. The tiny province now produces about 1.29 million tonnes of potatoes each year, about one-third of all the potatoes produced in Canada. So what better place to erect a giant potato than on beautiful P.E.I.?

The giant fibreglass spud — 4.27 metres tall and 2.1 metres wide — proudly stands at the entrance to the Prince Edward Island Potato Museum in O'Leary, about 110 kilometres northwest of Charlottetown.

Would You Believe Potato Fudge?

Yes, potato fudge! Here's a recipe for it from Spud Island, P.E.I.'s nickname.

240 mL (1 cup) hot, lump-free mashed potatoes
1 pinch of salt
30 mL (2 tablespoons) butter
950 mL (4 cups) icing sugar
950 mL (4 cups) unsweetened coconut
2.5 mL (1/2 teaspoon) vanilla extract
120 mL (1/2 cup) semi-sweet chocolate, melted
120 mL (1/2 cup) maraschino cherries, chopped
and drained (optional)
60 mL (1/4 cup) nuts (optional)

Spread the hot potatoes on the bottom of a large bowl and sprinkle the salt on them.
Spread the butter over the potatoes until it melts.
Add all the other ingredients except the chocolate, and mix them together well.
Press the mixture into a 23 x 33 centimetre (9" x 13") pan.
Drizzle the melted chocolate over the top.
Allow the fudge to set. (This may take a few hours.)
When it's hardened, cut into squares.

Bon appétit!

Eh –
What's that, eh?

Adding *eh* to show that you understand, as in "So, it's really far away, eh ..." or that you agree with what someone's just said, as in "Right on, eh" is a distinctly Canadian use of this two-letter English word. It's also used to connect parts of a "story" you're telling, as in, "First, I got my bike, eh, and then I took off, eh, and ..."

English speakers in Ontario, Manitoba and New Brunswick use it way more, eh, than people in the rest of the country. However, in 2007 a University of Toronto language researcher, Sali Tagliamonte, released a study, eh, and it showed that people in Toronto weren't using it very often anymore, especially not younger people.

So, *eh* may be on the way out, eh. But, then again, many newcomers like using it to sound really Canadian, eh. So you never know, eh, what'll happen to *eh* ...

Photo Credits